When I'm Feeling
SCARED

Written and illustrated by Trace Moroney

GINGHAM DOG
PRESS

Columbus, Ohio

When I'm feeling scared,
my heart beats so loud and fast
that I feel like it's going to burst
right out of my chest!

When I'm feeling scared,
my whole body trembles and shakes,
and my hair feels prickly.

Everyone feels scared sometimes.

Some things that make me
feel really scared are

creepy,
crawly
spiders

and bullies

and being alone in the dark.

It's okay to feel scared.
Feeling scared can help me stay away
from danger and make me yell out for…

HELP

Everyone is scared of different things.
Something that is scary to me
may not be scary to you.

Talking to someone
helps me understand
that what scared me

isn't so scary after all.

Sometimes I like to dress up
and *pretend* to be scary!

RRRUUGhh!

Think About It!

1. What does the little rabbit do when it feels scared?

2. What kinds of things make the little rabbit scared?

3. How do you know when the little rabbit is feeling scared?

4. What does the little rabbit do to feel better?

The Story and You!

1. What kinds of things make you feel scared?

2. What do you do when you feel scared?

3. On a separate piece of paper, draw a picture of something that makes you feel scared.

4. What makes you feel better?

For Mum and Dad

Text and illustration copyright © Trace Moroney
First published in Australia by The Five Mile Press Pty Ltd.
Printed in China.
This edition published in the United States in 2006 by
Gingham Dog Press, an imprint of School Specialty
Publishing, a member of the School Specialty Family.

Library of Congress Cataloging-in-Publication Data is on file
with the publisher.

Send all inquiries to:

School Specialty Publishing
8720 Orion Place
Columbus, OH 43240-2111

ISBN 0-7696-4427-9

1 2 3 4 5 6 7 8 9 FMP 10 09 08 07 06 05

www.SchoolSpecialtyPublishing.com